TAIWAN

ISLANDS IN THE SEA

William Russell

The Rourke Book Co., Inc.
Vero Beach, Florida 32964

Edited by Sandra A. Robinson

PHOTO CREDITS
All photos courtesy of Taiwan Information Division,
Coordination Council for North American Affairs

Library of Congress Cataloging-in-Publication Data

Russell, William, 1942-
    Taiwan / by William Russell.
        p. cm. — (Islands in the sea)
    Includes index.
    ISBN 1-55916-033-0
    1. Taiwan—Description and travel—Juvenile literature.
[1. Taiwan.] I. Title. II. Series.
DS799.24.R87   1994
951.24'9—dc20   93-48341
                                                      CIP
Printed in the USA   AC

TABLE OF CONTENTS

Taiwan   5
Forests and Mountains   6
Taiwan Long Ago   9
People of Taiwan   11
Living in Taiwan   14
Taipei   16
Visiting Taiwan   19
Taiwan's Farms   20
Map of Taiwan   21
Wildlife of Taiwan   22
Glossary   23
Index   24

TAIWAN

Sailors who saw Taiwan 400 years ago called it "the beautiful island." Much of Taiwan is still beautiful. The island has tall mountains, thick forests and green fields.

Taiwan lies in the South China Sea, 90 miles from the mainland of China.

Taiwan is also known as the Republic of China, or R.O.C. It is a separate nation from mainland China.

Mountainous Taiwan lies in the South China Sea, 90 miles from mainland China

FORESTS AND MOUNTAINS

Several islands make up Taiwan, just as several islands make up Hawaii. The main island of Taiwan is by far the largest. Taiwan is about the size of Connecticut and Massachusetts combined.

Blanketed with forests, Taiwan's mountains cover about half of the country. The tallest is Jade Mountain, 13,113 feet above **sea level.** Sixty-two other mountains in Taiwan stand more than 10,000 feet high.

Taiwan has a mild, sometimes hot climate. During certain times of the year, heavy rains and strong winds called **monsoons** strike Taiwan.

Green mountain forests cover much of Taiwan, which was once known as Formosa

TAIWAN LONG AGO

Taiwan's first settlers were Asian people who lived in tribes. About 1,500 years ago, some Chinese people moved onto Taiwan. Later, China claimed Taiwan as its territory.

In 1949, a civil war between the Chinese people ended. The Chinese Communists won the war. The Chinese Nationalists lost. Led by Chiang Kai-shek, they retreated to Taiwan. Taiwan then became the R.O.C.

Among Taiwan's nine tribes of native people are the Paiwans, dressed here in beads, silver ornaments and feathers

PEOPLE OF TAIWAN

For its small area, Taiwan has a large population — about 20 million people. About 325,000 are **native,** non-Chinese people who live in mountain villages. Most of the others are Chinese. Nine out of every 10 people on Taiwan can read and write Chinese, the native language.

Most Taiwanese live in the western part of the country. The land there is quite flat and good for farming.

Most of Taiwan's people are Chinese

Rubber rafts bob along the Hsiukulan River in the eastern coastal mountains of Taiwan

Festivals are an important part of the Chinese culture on Taiwan

LIVING IN TAIWAN

Most Taiwanese in large cities work in factories and shops. Taiwan's growing factories make products out of wood, steel, plastic and cloth. Many of these products are sold in the United States, Germany and Japan. People in cities dress like Americans in summer clothing.

Taiwanese who live in rural, or country, areas are usually farmers. They wear traditional Chinese clothing.

14

These Taiwanese people, eating with chopsticks, wear a mixture of Eastern (Chinese) and Western (European and American) clothing

TAIPEI

Taipei is the capital and most important city in Taiwan. Nearly 3 million Taiwanese live in this noisy, crowded and lively city. Many live in the city's high-rise apartments.

Several of Taiwan's factories are in and near Taipei. The nation's government and trade are based in Taipei.

However, not all of Taipei is modern. Temples, museums and festivals are reminders of old Taiwan.

Traffic rumbles into Taipei, Taiwan's capital city of 3 million people

VISITING TAIWAN

Visiting Taiwan is like seeing a small piece of China itself. The Chinese **culture,** or way of life, is very much a part of Taiwan.

Most Taiwanese practice Chinese customs. The art, food, religion and **architecture** of Taiwan are basically Chinese, too.

Visitors to Taiwan travel by cars, buses and trains. The modern east-west Cross Island Highway travels through exciting mountain scenery.

Taiwan's temples are built in the Chinese style

TAIWAN'S FARMS

Most of Taiwan is too **mountainous** for farming. Hundreds of thousands of farmers have to share the nation's small amount of farmland. Taiwanese farmers usually work on tiny farms of just two or three acres.

Many Taiwanese still use water buffaloes to plow the soil. Gasoline-powered equipment is slowly replacing buffalo power.

Taiwanese farms raise products such as tea, rice, bananas, mushrooms, ducks, chickens and hogs.

TAIWAN

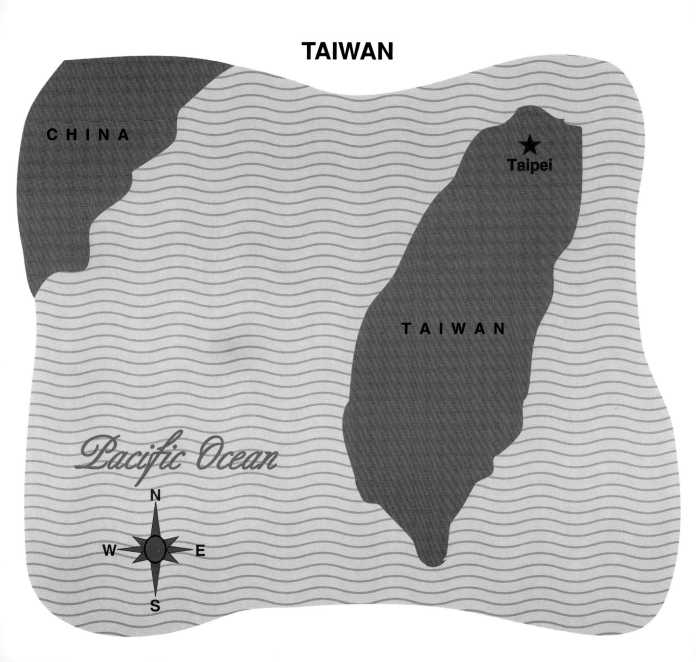

WILDLIFE OF TAIWAN

Several of Taiwan's wild animals have close cousins in North America. Taiwan, like North America, has pheasants, frogs, ducks, deer, bears, bats, salamanders, squirrels, otters, orioles, **martens** and egrets.

Several other Taiwanese animals are quite different from North American animals. These include scaly anteaters, mongooses, ferret badgers and the little leopard cats.

Clouded leopards once lived in Taiwan's mountain forests. Because of too much hunting, they may all be **extinct** — gone forever from Taiwan.

Glossary

architecture (ARK uh tek shur) — the type of design used in buildings built in a certain area or by a certain individual or group

culture (KULT cher) — a group of people's way of life

extinct (ex TINKT) — no longer existing

marten (MART in) — a tree-climbing member of the weasel and otter family; the marten resembles a large weasel

monsoon (mahn SOON) — a strong wind during certain seasons in southern Asia

mountainous (MOUNT in us) — referring to a place with mountains

native (NAY tihv) — referring to people, plants or animals that are *found naturally* in an area, and not people, plants or animals that are *brought into* an area

sea level (SEE LEHV uhl) — the same height, or level, as the sea

INDEX

architecture 19

art 19

Chiang Kai-shek 9

China 5, 9, 19

cities 14

climate 6

clothing 14

Cross Island Highway 19

culture 19

customs 19

factories 14, 16

farmers 14, 20

farming 11, 20

farmland 20

farms 20

festivals 16

food 19

forests 5, 6

Jade Mountain 6

leopards, clouded 22

map of Taiwan 21

monsoons 6

mountains 5, 6

museums 16

population 11

religion 19

South China Sea 5

Taipei 16

temples 16

tribes 9

water buffaloes 20

wild animals 22

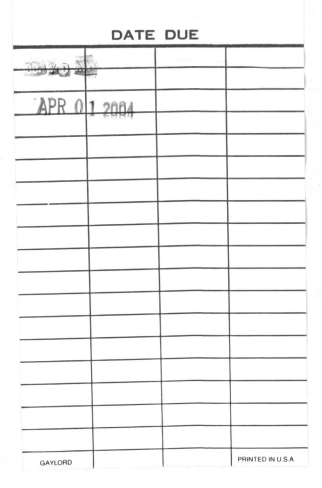

DATE DUE

APR 0 1 2004

GAYLORD   PRINTED IN U.S.A